Nature fact file

Wild Horses

Michael Bright
Consultant: Dr Nigel Dunstone, Durham University

southwater

This edition is published by Southwater

Southwater is an imprint of Anness Publishing Ltd
Hermes House, 88–89 Blackfriars Road, London SE1 8HA
tel. 020 7401 2077; fax 020 7633 9499
www.southwaterbooks.com; info@anness.com

© Anness Publishing Ltd 2001, 2003

UK agent: The Manning Partnership Ltd,
tel. 01225 478 444; fax 01225 478 440;
sales@manningpartnership.co.uk

UK distributor: Grantham Book Services Ltd, tel. 01476 541080; fax
01476 541061; orders@gbs.tbs-ltd.co.uk

North American agent/distributor: National Book Network, tel. 301 459
3366; fax 301 429 5746; www.nbnbooks.com

Australian agent/distributor: Pan Macmillan Australia, tel. 1300 135
113; fax 1300 135 103; customer.service@macmillan.com.au

Publisher: Joanna Lorenz
Managing Editor, Children's Books: Gilly Cameron Cooper
Project Editor: Rebecca Clunes
Editorial Assistant: Sarah Uttridge
Illustrators: Stuart Carter, Rob Sheffield
Production Controller: Claire Rae
Editorial Reader: Jonathan Marshall

10 9 8 7 6 5 4 3 2 1

PICTURE CREDITS
ABPL: Thomas Dressler: 18tl, 44tl, 45bl, 45cl, 45br;
AKG London: 15br, 29cr, 48tr; Ardea London: 37br, 47b, 49cr, 49t;
The Art Archive: 26t, 48bl; Australian War Memorial: 53cr; BBC
Natural History Unit: 8br, 17tr/ Karl Amman: 39cl/ John Cancalosi: 6tr,
2tl & 42t/ Alain Compost: 57t/ Richard Dutoit: 36tr/ Jeff Foott: 28t/
G & H Denzou: 31br, 3tr & 64tr/ Alistair Macewen: 13cr & 63tr/
Godfrey Merlon: 41tl/ Colin Preston: 46tr/ Anup Shah: 25c, 29tl, 35br,
37tr; Bruce Coleman Collection: 4br, 17br, 20bl, 38tl, 50br, 51tl, 55bl/
Jane Burton: 33tr/ Gerald Cubitt: 36bl/ Peter Davey: 39bl, 51tl/ Christer
Fredriksson: 9cl/ Steven Kaufman: 53bl & 62tr, 61cr/ Robert Maier: 6bl,
9tl, 25t, 24br, 32bl, 33tl, 33bl/ Dr Eckart Pott: 5tr, 8tl & 62br, 12bl,
37tl, 50tr/ Alan Potts: 48br/ Kim Taylor: 37bl/ Rod Williams: 60t/ Joseph
Van Wormer: 27t/ Gunter Ziesler: 58br; Mary Evans Picture Library:
5br, 11bl; Natural History Museum: M Long: 47cl, 47tr, 47cr; Only
Horses: 16tl, 17cl, 21br, 28bl, 42br, 42bl, 43cr, 43tl, 43tr; Kit
Houghton: 7tl, 9br, 10tr, 13br, 15tr, 18br, 22t, 24t, 32tr, 32br, 33br,
40b, 43b, 56tl; NHPA: 30t, 30cl, 30b, 31t, 31cl, 34bl, 40t/ Daryl
Balfour: 39br/ Nigel Dennis: 44b/ Yves Lanceau: 14bl/ Christophe Ratier:
16bl/ Alan Williams 15cl/ Norbert Wu: 38b; Oxford Scientific Films:
15bl, 41cl, 53br, 54cr, 61bl, 61t/ Alan & Sandy Carey: 14tl/ Martyn
Chillmaid: 8bl/ Martin Colbeck: 29b/ Martin Cordano: 41cr/ Eastcott/
Momatiuk: 7bl & 62bl, 29cl, 30tr/ Michael Fogden: 2b, 50bl & 63cl/
Carol Geake: 25bl/ Dave Hamman: 59bl/ Mike Hill: 59tr/ Isaac
Kehimkar: 53tl/ Alistair Macewen: 24bl/ Ben Osborne: 19t/ William
Paton: 55br/ Kjell Sandved: 34br/ Anup Shah 7tr, 52bl/ David Tipling:
4-5, 21bl/ Philip Tull: 11cr/ Tom Ulrich: 23br/ Fred Whitehead: 11br,
3br & 60bl, 1 & 61br; Planet Earth Pictures: 19bl, 20tr, 21cl, 23b,
27br, 31bl, 45tl, 52t, 59tl/ Richard Coomber: 7br/ Wendy Dennis:
45t/ Georgette Douwma: 18bl/ Yva Momatiuk: 5cr/ Jonathan P. Scott
23cl/ Anup Shah: 39tr; South African Museum: 55t/ Tony Stone:
14br, 26b, 27bl, 27r & 64bl/ Eastcott/ Momatiuk: 19br, 22b, 23t,
41br; Warren Photographic: Jane Burton: 51b; Zoological Society of
London: 54bl, 54tl

T E N T S

Saved from Extinction

Wild horses once ranged throughout the world. Climate change reduced their numbers until they almost became extinct. However, about 6,000 years ago, horses were tamed by people. Through breeding, many shapes and sizes of horse developed to serve different human needs. Horses became essential to human society, and as a result, they are found all over the world again.

Domestic and wild horses are a single species (*Equus caballus*). They belong to a larger family known as equids. Asses and zebras are also equids, and very closely related to horses. The three groups evolved different characteristics that enabled them to survive in particular habitats. Wild horses lived on the open steppes of central Asia and zebras moved to the grasslands of southern Africa. Asses moved into hot desert lands.

long neck for grazing on the ground

large eyes, ears and nostrils for detecting predators

prominent mane of coarser hair on the back of the neck

coat of tightly packed, weatherproof hair

powerful legs — where a horse's main strength lies — particularly in the hindlimbs

◀ **ZEBRA STRIPES**
All three species of zebra—the plains (*Equus burchelli*), mountain (*E. zebra*) and Grevy's (*E. grevyi*)—live in Africa. All zebras have a unique pattern of stripes so other zebras in the herd can recognise it.

▲ **FREE FERAL HORSES**
Mustangs are "feral" horses that roam in parts of North America. Feral describes horses that are descended from domestic animals that were turned loose or escaped and have reverted to the wild.

▼ HORSE HIGHLIGHTS

Przewalski's horse (*Equus ferus przewalskii*) from Mongolia is the last true species of wild horse. It has an large head and squat body, but its general shape is shared by all equids. Although extinct in the wild, it survived in captivity and has been returned to the wild in nature reserves.

long tail, useful for swatting flies

▶ DESERT ASSES

The Persian onager (*Equus hemionus*) is a type of Asian wild ass that lives in Iran. It is very rare. The typical ass-shape is more compact than that of a horse. There are two other ass species, the kiang (*E. kiang*) from Tibet and the African wild ass (*E. asinus*). All asses live in desert regions.

▶ ROAMING FREE

These horses are "semi-wild." Although they are owned by people, the horses are turned loose for most of the year and are left to range freely over a wide area.

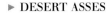

A Symbol of Purity

Ancient myths tell of beautiful, pure white horses with a single, magical horn. These gentle and shy creatures of fairy tales and legends came to be known as unicorns. The unicorn's first recorded appearance is on Assyrian stonework of 3,400 years ago. This may have been inspired by an animal described by early travelers from the East—the Indian rhinoceros! The unicorn resurfaced in the writings of ancient Greeks, and in medieval myths. Traditionally, it is depicted with a spiral tusk like that of a narwhal (a type of whale), a lion's tail and cloven feet like a goat's.

Shapes and Sizes

Equids take their place in the animal world as medium-sized plant eaters. Their heads and necks are long to suit a grazing lifestyle. Their bodies range in shape from the stocky zebras, with their broad heads and short legs, to the slender-headed, long-limbed Arab breed of domestic horse.

Truly wild horses and zebras stand 3–4 feet tall at the shoulder. Domestic horses vary greatly in size because they have been bred for particular purposes. A shire horse, bred for heavy farm work, can stand up to 5 feet tall. They weigh around 1 ton, and can pull up to 50 tons in weight. New miniature horse breeds may be the size of a large dog. Fully grown mares (female horses)—both domestic and wild—are usually about 10 percent smaller than stallions (male horses).

▲ **SCOTTISH MINIATURE**

Shetland ponies are one of the smallest breeds of horse and very hardy. They have stocky bodies and short legs and range in height from 2 to 3 feet. The ponies have lived semi-wild on the storm-lashed Shetland Isles off the Scottish coast for 2,000 years. Their diet is heather, rough grass and seaweed. In the 1800s, many were put to work in coal mines because they are small but remarkably strong.

▼ **GERMAN GIANT**

The Schwarzwälder Kaltblut or Black Forest heavy horse is a robust working horse standing up to 5¼ feet at the shoulder. It was bred to pull plows and wagons before tractors and trucks appeared. It is also tough and can withstand the harsh conditions in mountain regions. Today, the Schwarzwälder is rare, but can be found pulling sleighs at ski resorts.

◀ COWBOY CARRIER

Criollo horses were bred from *baguales*, the feral horses of the Pampas grasslands in Argentina. These in turn were descended from Spanish horses that escaped from or were abandoned by explorers in the 1500s. Strong, agile and medium-sized at about 5 feet, they make ideal mounts for cowboys and polo players.

AFRICAN ANCESTOR

The Nubian subspecies of the African wild ass stands up to 4¾ feet tall at the shoulder. It is thought to be the ancestor of the domestic donkey. Fully grown donkeys can be between 3 feet tall and up to the size of a horse, depending on the breed.

▼ BORN IN THE USA

American mustangs are medium-sized with a strong build, like the Spanish horses they are descended from. Their feet have evolved a special adaptation called a mule foot. The sole is concave, like that of a mule, to avoid getting bruised on rocky terrain.

▲ LINK TO THE PAST

Grevy's zebra is the largest wild equid. It may weigh nearly twice as much as a plains zebra. With its narrow stripes, large head, slender build and long legs, it is thought to resemble the common ancestor of all equids.

Coats and Grooming

Horses have coats of tightly packed hairs that provide protection against the weather. Wild horses and asses are usually colored gray or brown above and white below, blending in with the plains and deserts where they live. Many have a dark stripe running the length of their spine. Some, such as the African ass, have stripes on their legs, while zebras have stripes all over.

Wild equids have an erect mane of coarse hair. Its function is unclear, but it may provide some protection against biting insects and the weather. The tail is certainly used as a fly swatter. Horses have long tails of loose hair, while asses and zebras have tails ending with tufts of hair.

▲ KEEPING WARM
The length of a horse's hair varies according to where it lives. Horses that live in cold climates, such as this Dartmoor pony, have long hair and a thick mane. Horses often shed their heavy winter coats in spring. Equids in hot countries, such as the wild ass and zebra, have short hair all year around.

▲ SCRATCH AN ITCH
All horses and asses must go into great contortions to scratch some of the more inaccessible parts of their body. This khur, a type of ass from north west India, uses its hind leg to scratch its neck.

▲ SOCIAL GROOMING
All equids groom each other, picking off fleas and ticks. Grooming keeps the coat in good condition by removing loose hair and dead skin. It also strengthens relationships.

◄ **IT'S A ROLL OVER**
Wallowing in grass, dust and dry or damp sand is one way horses keep their coats in good condition. It also helps remove dandruff and reduce external parasites such as blood-sucking ticks. Unlike cattle, all equids can roll over completely.

▲ **GROOMING NIBBLE**
A Camargue horse grooms its legs by nibbling its skin with its teeth. Just above the knee, on the inside of each leg, all equids have a wart-like, hairless callus. These are known as chestnuts. Their function is unknown.

HELPING HAND ►
Equids scratch the parts they cannot reach with teeth or hooves by rubbing against trees and rocks. There is often a line at popular scratching posts. Who goes first depends on social rank in the herd.

9

Built for Speed

Equids are designed to be able to flee from predators. Their skeletons are lightweight, strong and geared for maximum speed with minimum energy. A horse's upper leg bones, for example, are fused into a single, strong bone, while in humans, their equivalents are two separate bones. The joints are less flexible than those of a human. Instead, they are strong in an up-and-down direction to support and protect powerful tendons and muscles. A horse's skeleton is designed to absorb the weight and impact of its body as it moves over the ground.

▲ RESTING ON AUTOMATIC

When equids are standing at rest, the patella (kneecap) slots into a groove in the femur (leg bone). This locks their back legs into an energy-saving position, just like our knees. Another mechanism keeps the horse's head from dropping to the ground. A ligament in the neck acts like a piece of elastic, returning the head to an upright resting position when the horse is not grazing.

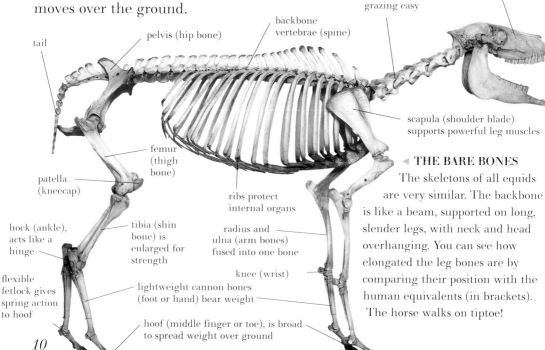

long neck vertebrae make grazing easy

long, narrow skull

backbone vertebrae (spine)

pelvis (hip bone)

tail

scapula (shoulder blade) supports powerful leg muscles

femur (thigh bone)

◀ THE BARE BONES
The skeletons of all equids are very similar. The backbone is like a beam, supported on long, slender legs, with neck and head overhanging. You can see how elongated the leg bones are by comparing their position with the human equivalents (in brackets). The horse walks on tiptoe!

patella (kneecap)

ribs protect internal organs

hock (ankle), acts like a hinge

tibia (shin bone) is enlarged for strength

radius and ulna (arm bones) fused into one bone

knee (wrist)

flexible fetlock gives spring action to hoof

lightweight cannon bones (foot or hand) bear weight

hoof (middle finger or toe), is broad to spread weight over ground

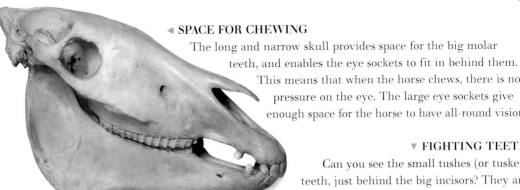

◀ **SPACE FOR CHEWING**

The long and narrow skull provides space for the big molar teeth, and enables the eye sockets to fit in behind them. This means that when the horse chews, there is no pressure on the eye. The large eye sockets give enough space for the horse to have all-round vision.

▼ **FIGHTING TEETH**

Can you see the small tushes (or tusker) teeth, just behind the big incisors? They are used in fights between stallions. Females have very small tushes teeth or none at all.

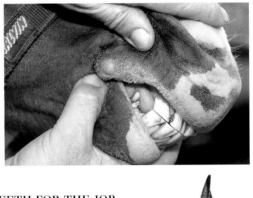

Pegasus

Greek mythology tells of a winged horse called Pegasus. He appeared from the blood of the evil Medusa when she was beheaded. Pegasus was ridden by the hero Bellerophon. Together they defeated the fire-breathing monster, the Chimera. Bellerophon tried to ride Pegasus to heaven but the gods were angry and he was thrown off and killed. Pegasus became a constellation in the night sky.

▶ **TEETH FOR THE JOB**

Mare have 36-40 teeth and stallions 44 teeth. A horse's teeth are specially adapted for its diet. Chisel-shaped incisors at the front snip through grass. Molars in the side of the mouth grind down the grass before it is swallowed. The degree of wear on teeth is sometimes used to calculate a horse's age. This can be misleading, as some foods wear down the teeth more than others do.

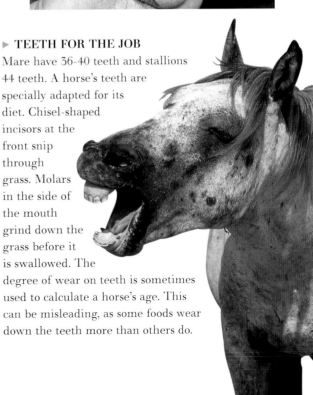

Body Power

The horse is one of the fastest long-distance runners in the animal world. Its digestive system processes large quantities of food in order to extract sufficient energy. The digestive system is in two parts. The food is partly digested in the stomach, then moves quickly through to the hindgut (the cecum, the large colon and the small colon). Here, bacteria break down the cell walls of the plants. The nutrients are released, and special cells lining the gut are ready to absorb them.

Equids also have a big heart and large lungs. This allows them to run quickly and over a long distance. The bigger the heart, the faster the horse.

Elastic tendons are another specialty. Together with the joints and ligaments, they stretch and give like elastic to conserve energy and cushion impact on the ground when the horse is on the move.

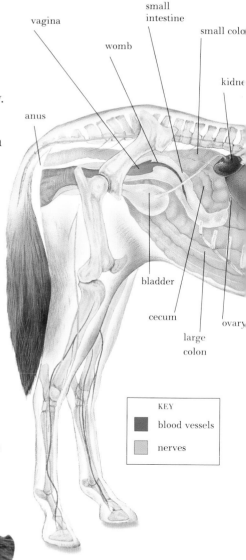

small intestine

vagina

womb

small colo

kidne

anus

bladder

cecum

large colon

ovary

KEY

blood vessels

nerves

◀ FLEXIBLE LIPS
The horse's mobile, sensitive lips are described as prehensile (able to grasp). They are used to select and pick food. When a horse wants to use its power of smell to full effect, it curls its lips back.

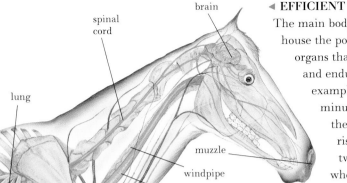

brain

spinal
cord

lung

muzzle

windpipe

esophagus

heart

liver

stomach

spleen

◄ EFFICIENT BODYWORKS

The main body of the horse is big enough to house the powerful muscles and large organs that the animal needs for speed and endurance. The large heart, for example, pumps at 30-40 beats per minute when resting—about half the rate of a human's. This can rise to a top rate of 240—nearly twice the rate of a human's—when working hard. This means that blood circulates around the body very efficiently.

► ONE WAY TRIP

Horses eat almost continuously, and have an extra-long digestive tract—around 100 feet—to get as much benefit as possible from their low-grade diet. They cannot vomit because one-way valves in the stomach prevent food from being regurgitated. Eating something poisonous could, therefore, be fatal.

► MUSCLE POWER

Large masses of muscle enable horses to move quickly over long distances and to use their limbs in the most efficient way. Cheek muscles are extra-powerful too, to grind down tough food.

Movement and Resting

▲ **THE TROT**
Once a horse reaches a certain walking speed, it becomes more energy-saving to trot. In order to go faster, the feet leave the ground to incorporate little springs forward into the gait. Top trotting speed is about 8 miles per hour for the average equid.

The way in which a horse moves makes the most of its energy reserves. The main thrust comes from the hind legs. The forelegs cushion jolts during running and jumping. Equids have four distinctive gaits—the walk, the two-beat trot, the three-beat canter and the four-beat gallop. Each is designed to conserve energy at different speeds.

The hooves of wild and domestic horses are quite broad. This spreads weight over a wider area so that the hoof does not dig into the ground. Equids that live in rocky or mountainous areas, such as the Asiatic wild horse and the mountain zebra, have narrower hooves for sure footedness.

▲ **THE CANTER**
A cantering horse has a rocking gait and moves at 9 to 12 miles per hour. The legs move one after the other in a smooth action. Horses canter to cover distances quickly, perhaps when moving to a waterhole.

▲ **THE GALLOP**
The gallop is a horse's fastest gait, used when escaping predators. Horses and asses can gallop up to speeds of 30 miles per hour. The gallop is designed for stability and best use of energy. The animal stretches its limbs to their limits, making a smooth action that reduces the shock of hitting the ground at speed.

▶ SWIMMING

A herd of semi-wild horses in Portugal wades and swims across a wide river. All equids can swim. Even foals can swim from very early days, though they keep close to protective mares.

◀ NURSERY NAP

A foal rests on its side with its limbs extended. Foals lie down more frequently than adults. Horses usually rest standing up because their heart and lungs have to work harder when they are lying down.

▼ BEDTIME

This herd of Przewalski's horses is resting. In any 24-hour period, a horse is alert for about 19 hours, drowsy for two and asleep for three. Sleep is taken in short bursts. Equids do not sleep for long periods as they need to be alert to predators.

Rakahsh

The legendary Persian hero Rustam had a horse called Rakahsh, who was renowned for his speed and strength. Their adventures are told in the Book of Kings, *an 11th-century epic poem. Among many stories of the horse's bravery is the tale of a lion attacking the Persian camp. Rakahsh killed the lion and saved the day.*

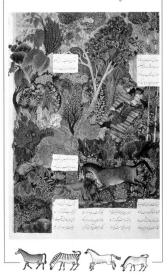

The White

STRONG FEATURES
A pair of young stallions having a play fight show off some of the Camargue horse's best features. Their striking white coats are silky in texture, and their manes and tails are long. The neck is short and the hindquarters are solid and powerful.

In a marshy area of southern France called the Camargue, herds of white horses have run free for over 1,000 years. They are the semi-wild descendants of domestic horses, and are known as "the white horses of the sea". Their origins may go back to prehistoric times, as 15,000-year-old cave paintings of very similar horses have been found nearby. When Roman and Saracen invaders came into the region, they crossbred their war horses with those they found in the Camargue.

Since 1968, Camargue horses have been a recognized breed. More than 500 run wild there. Once a year, they are rounded up and branded. Some are tamed by *guardiens* (cowboys) to ride in the traditional roundups of the black Camargue bulls.

LIVING TOGETHER
Several breeding groups may move around as one big herd, especially in summer. There are up to 30 semi-wild herds, or *manades*, and 500-600 horses altogether. Each breeding group is made up of a stallion, mares, fillies and colts up to three years old.

Horses of the Sea

MARSH NEIGHBORS

Wetland birds called egrets settle on the horses' backs, ready to pounce on insects or frogs disturbed by their hooves. The birds sometimes act as an early warning system of danger, when they suddenly fly away. Flamingoes and black bulls also live on the marshes.

FOOD FOR ALL SEASONS

A mare grazes with her foal on the stunted, saltmarsh vegetation. Foals are born brown or dark grey, but become white as they grow older. Reeds are the main diet in spring and summer. In winter, the ground may freeze, and the horses paw it with their hooves to loosen the sparse vegetation and roots. They have also been known to graze with their muzzles under water.

STEPPING OUT

The Camargue horse walks with a long, high-stepping stride. It trots rarely and awkwardly, but is agile and has a free, open canter and gallop. The hooves are broader than those of other breeds and less likely to sink into marshy ground.

17

Intelligence and Senses

The horse has a relatively large brain that interprets information from its well-developed senses. As a result, equids have excellent memories, a brilliant sense of direction and an extraordinary ability to sense mood and danger. The senses work together in other ways too. Eyes are set well back on each side of the skull, giving almost all-around vision. But there is a blind spot directly behind the head. To cover this, the horse swivels its ears right around, and switches over to its sense of hearing. Only when horses look straight ahead do both eyes operate together to give binocular vision. Then, it can see three-dimensional images and judge distances. This enables them to jump obstacles with great accuracy.

▲ **CHECK IT OUT**
A stallion uses its excellent sense of smell to check out deposits of dung and urine from another herd. He will find out how recently the other herd passed by, if it contains a mare in heat and if the herd is led by a stallion.

GATHERING SMELLS ▶
Curling back its lips in this way is a horse's reaction to unfamiliar smells. It is known as the flehmen reaction, and it is also used to identify females who are in a receptive sexual state. With its acute sense of smell, a horse can be alerted to predators and detect subtle changes in food quality.

▲ **THE TASTE TEST**
Little is known about a horse's sense of taste, although it is likely to be fairly sensitive. This can be seen from the way it grazes, pushing aside some plants to reach others. Taste may also be involved when horses groom each other.

▲ CLEVER HORSE

Memory is important for survival. Remembering where water or food can be found and which plants are good to eat may be a matter of life or death for a wild horse. Horses do well in intelligence and memory tests. In one test, horses were taught to recognize patterns. When they were tested a year later they could remember almost all, a score far better than most humans could do.

▼ SHARP EYES

A horse can see objects clearly at short and long distances at the same time because they register on different areas of the eye. This is useful for keeping watch for predators while grazing. (Human eyes have variable focus that automatically adjusts to distances.) A horse can see better than a cat or a dog during daylight, and its nighttime vision is also very good.

◄ ALERT EARS

All equids have ears that behave rather like radar dishes. They can turn in the direction of a sound quite independently of each other, while the rest of the body remains still. The rotating action is operated by no fewer than 16 muscles. This, together with the large size of the outer ear, means that a horse's sense of hearing is far more acute than a human's.

Eating for Energy

Wild horses graze for about 16 hours a day, from early in the morning until around midnight. In hot countries, asses and zebras graze from dawn until late morning, rest during the hottest part of the day, and then graze again until late afternoon. All equids are vegetarian and have adapted to making the most of low-grade food, mainly grass.

The nutrients in grass are difficult for an animal's body to extract. Equids solve the problem by having an extra-long digestive system, and by pushing as much food as they can through their bodies. The food converts to energy in as short a time as possible. Horses nibble vegetation with their front incisor teeth, then grind it down with their molars before swallowing. It's a virtually nonstop cycle of eating, digesting and producing waste. Equids can survive on food of a poorer quality than cattle can.

▲ CHEW WELL!
A slow, deliberate style of eating ensures that food is thoroughly ground down. Cows have an extra stomach to help break food down, but horses have only one. This means that equids must chew slowly and wash the food down with plenty of saliva to aid digestion.

◄ HARD TIMES
Cold weather has made the ground hard, and snow covers the scant winter vegetation. These horses must paw at the ground to uncover the grass and dig up roots. They may even eat tree bark. Weak horses may not survive a hard winter.

STRESS IN THE STABLE ▶

When domestic horses are brought into stables they are fed well but often only three times a day. This is very different from a horse's natural feeding pattern, which is continuous and varied grazing. Bored stabled horses sometimes develop "vices," such as crib-chewing, tongue swallowing and rug-chewing. Although a horse may be given nutritious fodder, it is starved of its natural behavior.

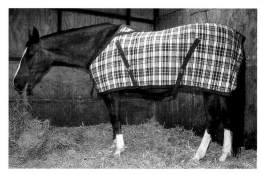

◀ SURVIVAL IN DRY LAND

Grevy's zebras live in dry thornbush country. If water is scarce, they migrate to the highlands. If water and grazing remains available, however, they stay and survive on grasses, or even bushes, that are too tough for other herbivores to eat. They dig water holes—and defend them fiercely.

▲ ALTERNATIVE FOODS

A semi-wild horse from the New Forest, England, uses its flexible lips to pick some gorse flowers. Horses often choose more interesting foods than grass when they are available. They push out unwanted bits with their tongue.

▲ WATERHOLE

Wild horses drink daily, although they can go without water for long periods of time. Most animals only drink fresh water. Wild asses, Grevy's and mountain zebras can tolerate brackish (stale, salty) water. This gives them a better chance of surviving droughts than fellow grazers, such as antelope.

Social Life

All equids are herd animals. Horses, plains and mountain zebras form what is described as a "stable" herd. Each member of the herd knows everyone else. The groups are strictly structured, with each animal knowing its place. There is a single stallion with a harem of mares and their foals. Stable herds do not identify with a particular territory.

Wild asses and Grevy's zebras have a loose, or "unstable" herd structure. They live in dry habitats where individual dominant males defend territories that contain water and food. Females live in unstable groups, usually with related animals or with those of the same social status. They enter the territories of resident males to feed and drink, and so join their herds temporarily.

▲ **LEARNING BEHAVIOR**
A foal learns its first lessons on survival from its mother. In a process called imprinting, foals bond to the animal they see most often, which is usually their mother, within a few days of being born. They later learn from watching other members of the herd.

▶ **BACHELOR BOYS**
Mustang colts have banded together in a bachelor group. At two to three years, they are old enough to form a threat to the reigning stallion, and have been driven from their herd. Lone stallions find survival difficult away from the herd.

▲ FERAL ORDER
This group of mustangs consists of a dominant stallion, six mares and a foal. The foal will have the same social status as its mother until it grows up. A filly may remain with the same herd, or she may be attracted away or kidnapped by a rival stallion to join his herd.

◀ SOCIAL RISE
Each member of a herd of plains zebras has its position in the pecking order. Recently recruited mares are the least important. As they gain experience over time, though, they can climb the social ladder.

▶ FEMALE POWER
Like all semi-wild horses, these Icelandic ponies form a stable herd. It is usually the dominant mare who decides where to graze and when to move. The stallion keeps the group together and prevents mares from leaving the herd.

◀ SEASONAL CHANGE
Khurs live in the desert in small groups for most of the year. During the wet season there is more food, and khurs gather in larger groups of up to 50. They mate at this time of year.

Communication

Because horses are social animals that live in herds, they need to communicate with each other. They have a wide range of expressive behavior ranging from sounds and smells to a complex body language.

Animals recognize each other by their appearance and smell, and certain sounds are common to all equids. The short whinny is a warning call, while the long version is a sign of contentment. Contact and territorial calls vary with each species. Horses whinny, asses bray, Grevy's zebras "bell" (so called because the sound is said to resemble a deep bell), mountain zebras whistle, and plains zebras bark. Horses, asses and zebras recognize and react to the calls of all other species of equids but do not respond to the calls of cattle or antelope.

▲ ON YOUR GUARD!
This horse has flattened its ears back in a threatening posture. It is showing its dominance without resorting to a fight. Ears flattened to the side may also indicate boredom or tiredness.

▲ BABY TALK
Young horses show respect to their elders by holding their ears to the side, displaying their teeth and making chewing movements. This is not a sign that the foal might bite, but is rather like preparing for a mutual grooming session. It's a way of saying "I'm friendly."

▲ TAKING NOTE
Horses are alert to the signals of others in their herd. If one horse is curious about something, its ears will prick forward, and the rest of the herd will take an interest.

◀ MUTUAL GROOMING

Horses, like all other equids, will nibble a favorite partner, grooming those places they cannot reach for themselves. The amount of time two horses spend grooming each other shows how friendly they are. Grooming helps to keep a herd together, and it occurs even when coats are in perfect condition.

▶ FRIENDLY GREETING

When members of a herd meet up, they welcome each other with a series of greeting rituals. They may stretch heads, touch and sniff noses, push each other and then part. Good friends may lay their heads on each other's backs.

◀ WILD AT HEART

Mares often develop personal bonds with other horses in the herd. For domestic horses, this is usually with close relatives, such as sisters or adult daughters. In feral horses, these bonds are more likely to develop between unrelated mares. In all herds, the bonds are less strong in groups led by a stallion, because he becomes the mares' center of attention.

Mustangs of the

BATTLE OF WILLS
Native North Americans captured and tamed feral horses for hunting and fighting. The riding skills of the Plains tribes in particular made the most of the mustang's toughness and agility.

ANCESTRAL LOOK
The mustang's strong profile and long, thick mane are inherited from its Spanish ancestors. The Spanish horses, similar to today's Andalucian breed, were considered the finest in Europe in the 1400s.

Wild horses died out in the Americas 10,000 years before Spanish invaders arrived with their fine, sturdy mounts in the 1500s. The Aztecs of Central America thought that the mounted Spanish soldiers were half man, half beast.

Spanish Settlers in North America kept horses, but many escaped or were abandoned. They formed wild herds and survived well. The mountains and plains, desert and chaparral scrubland were not unlike the horses' ancestral homeland in southern Spain.

Many mustangs have distinctive features inherited from their ancestors. These include hooked "fox ears," a rattling snort and "glass" (blue colored) eyes.

The feral mustang has provided the base for many distinctive American breeds.

Wild West

SAFETY IN NUMBERS
Neighboring groups of mustangs band together to flee from danger. A typical herd consists of a stallion, a few mares and their colts. The word mustang comes from *mestena*, the Spanish for a herd of horses. American Indians particularly liked the "painted" (two-color) horses like those above.

TOUGH LIFE
The mustangs of the mountains endure polar conditions in winter. Other herds have adapted to the heat of the scrubland and desert.

PREDATORS
Something has startled this group. However, the mustang's only predators are the mountain lion or puma—and humans. Today there are about 30,000 wild mustangs. At the end of the 1700s, there were millions. Over the next 200 years, they were hunted and shot, and slaughtered for dogfood. Today, many herds are protected.

FRIENDS FOR NOW
Young stallions often form small bachelor groups. If fillies should join the group, one stallion fights to become the dominant harem master and drives the others away.

Combat

Horses, zebras and asses prefer to settle disputes before coming to blows. Minor differences are settled with threatening postures. Equids display their willingness to fight without actually doing so. Occasionally, fights are inevitable. Male horses, plains and mountain zebras will fight over possession of a mare or harem. Grevy's zebras and wild asses fight prime territory.

Fights can be very dramatic, but the combatants tend not to hurt others of their own species. Rather than injure the opponent, the object is to make him lose his balance. The animal remaining upright is the victor.

▲ **REAR IN ANGER**
These mustang stallions are at the most dramatic stage in a fight. They rear up on their hind legs, and strike out with the forelegs. They will try to bite their opponent's ears, neck and throat.

◄ **COMING TO BLOWS**
Stallion fights are dramatic but rarely bloody. Bites are painful, however, and the stallion's small canine teeth can cause particular damage. If things get out of hand, the weaker animals can flee. In paddocks, where domestic animals cannot escape, stallion fights have been known to end in death.

▲ KICK OFF

Females rebuff the unwelcome attention of a stallion or the irritating advances of a neighbor by kicking out with the hind feet. Zebras' hooves are quite sharp. A zebra can also use this kick to defend itself from predators, such as lions, and inflict lasting damage.

The Trojan Horse

The ancient Greeks had held the city of Troy under siege for months, but they could not break the city defences. Eventually, they built a gigantic wooden horse. It was so big, they were able to fill it with soldiers. The Greeks then pretended to retreat, leaving the horse behind. The Trojans hauled it inside the city. That night the Greek soldiers broke out of the horse, opened the city gates and Troy was taken.

▼ FIGHT DANCE

These zebras are showing "circling" combat. They move round one another, attempting to bite their opponent's legs, while at the same time avoiding the other's teeth. The defence tactic is to fold the legs under the body and sink to the knees.

▲ NECK FIGHTING

Disputes are sometimes settled by a neck fight. Each combatant attempts to raise its neck above its opponent's neck and press down the other's head. This will establish which is the dominant animal while avoiding any serious damage.

A Foal

In the wild, foals are born when there is plenty of food and water around, and the weather is not too extreme. This will be in spring in temperate climates, such as northern Europe, and in the wet season in the tropics. The breeding season is usually brief. The foals have a greater chance of survival from predators if they are all born at the same time, rather than in ones or twos throughout the year.

In a stable, family herd, such as that of plains zebras, a pregnant female stays in her group when she gives birth. The stallion stands guard nearby. In the territorial herds of wild asses and Grevy's zebras, a mare may be on her own. If she is disturbed or in danger, she is able to delay the birth.

1 Some mares lie on their side during foaling, while others remain standing. The foal emerges head first, with its forelegs extended. It only takes a few minutes for it to be born. At first it is still enclosed in the caul in which it developed in the womb. But it soon breaks free of the caul by shaking itself or standing up.

2 The placenta, through which the foal received nutrients when it was still in the womb, comes out immediately after the birth. The mother might chew on this but she does not eat it.

3 The mother licks the newborn foal all over, especially under the tail. This stimulates it to produce its first feces. Licking establishes the maternal bond. From now on, the mother will be able to recognize her foal from all others. It will take about a week for the foal to recognize its mother.

is Born

4 The newborn foal struggles to its feet. It will stand up within ten minutes of birth, and will soon be able to canter. The foal's first few days of life are taken up with feeding, practicing to use its legs and napping. Feeds last for a few minutes each, and a rest may be between 20 minutes and one hour long.

5 The mother is very aggressive at this time. She chases other horses away and may even bite them. This ensures that the foal will imprint on her (recognize her as its source of food and protection) rather than any other animal in the herd. After about a week, the mare calms down, and the foal is allowed to meet with others of its own kind.

Instinct tells this plains zebra foal that its mother's teats are found between the legs and the belly, but it might search between the forelegs before finding the right spot. Foals drink their mother's milk for about a year.

This khur foal might live for 35 years — the average lifespan of all wild equids. For the first two years it will stay with its mother. Asses usually foal every two years, but horses and zebras sometimes have one foal a year, if conditions are good.

Growing Up

A wild foal must use the period it spends close to its mother to learn how to eventually survive without her. The foal often bursts into life, prancing, running, leaping about and kicking its back feet into the air for no obvious reason. It looks to be having a wonderful time, but it does not make these exaggerated movements for fun. The behavior is known as 'play', but it is highly serious. It ensures that the foal's body is toned up and that nerves and muscles are working together. If predators should attack, the foal needs to be able to escape rapidly. Young domestic horses will show the same anti-predator movements, even though they are rarely chased.

▲ **AWAY FROM THE HERD**
A foal is rarely left alone for long. Its mother is always nearby, keeping an eye on it. When it is about six months old, a domestic horse is weaned and separated from its mother. Wild and feral horses are weaned at 8–13 months old, when the youngster is rejected by its mother. It is old enough to fend for itself.

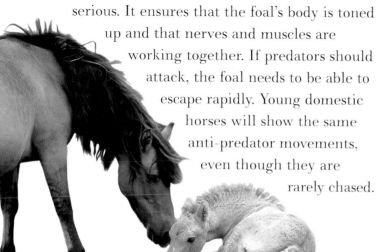

▲ **FAMILY SCENT**
This Dartmoor pony mother and foal recognize each other primarily by smell. Identities were established when the foal was newly born. The youngster remains close to its mother for many months, during which time it will learn what is good to eat, what is dangerous and how to behave in horse society.

PLAYFIGHTING FOALS ▶
A foal's place in the hierarchy (pecking order) is determined partly by its mother's rank, and partly by its ability to do well in a friendly fight with other foals, known as a 'playfight'. Colts playfight to prepare for the real thing. As stallions they fight to try to take over and retain their own herd.

NEW ARRIVAL IN SARDINIA

This mother and foal live wild on the Giara plateau in Sardinia. They are small horses, growing no bigger than 4ft high at the withers (shoulder). Sardinian horses have a large head and sad, almond-shaped eyes.

EXPLORING THE ENVIRONMENT

Open water would be frightening to a foal, but this Welsh pony foal, in the Brecon Beacons National Park in Wales, is shown by its mother that it need not be afraid. If they should chance upon deeper water, foals are able to swim not long after they can walk.

MORE FOOD, PLEASE

This colt foal seeks attention by pawing its mother's back. It is probably hungry and wants its mother to stand so it can feed on her milk. Foals demand milk every few hours for their first month or two. Later, young horses imitate their mother as she feeds, and sample green foods, such as grasses and herbs.

RACING AWAY FROM DANGER ▶

Foals are born with the ability to run fast so that they are able to keep up with the rest of the herd when they flee from predators. Feral horses, like these in New Zealand, tend to be very alert and can be frightened by the simplest thing, such as a piece of paper flapping in the wind.

World View

Zebras and asses live in both temperate and dry, tropical regions. They roam over open landscapes such as the savannahs (grasslands) of Africa and the rocky plains and dry scrubland of Asia. Their range in these areas is limited by the extent of human settlement on their habitats.

Zebras are only found in Africa, south of the Sahara Desert. There are isolated populations of wild asses in eastern Africa, the Middle East and India.

Feral horses occur in many parts of the world, wherever they have been released by or have escaped from people. Semi-wild herds are allowed to run free in many European countries, where large tracts of open country are left unfenced.

NORTH
AMERICA

1   8

2

3

SOUTH
AMERICA

4

◀ **AUSTRALIA**
Brumbies are found in a wide range of habitats throughout Australia. They run wild over dry plains, wetlands, grasslands and in the mountains. Australia has the largest number of feral horses in the world.

▼ **SOUTH AMERICA**
These feral horses live on the Falkland Islands, near Argentina. They were taken there by the French in 1764. Their home is one of bleak moorland, sand-dunes and rocks.

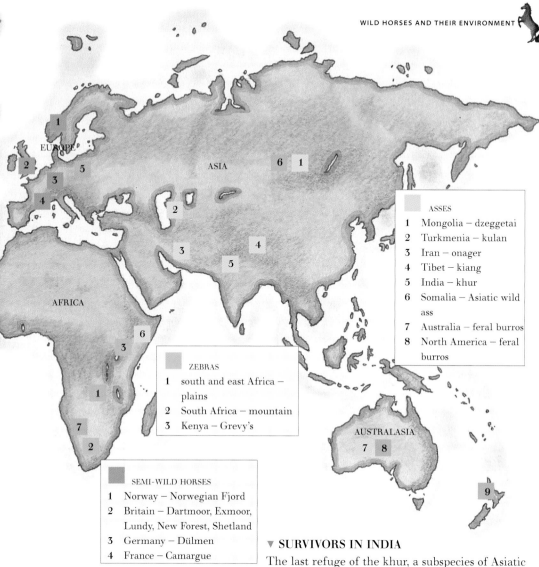

EUROPE

ASIA

6 1

2

3

4

5

2

3

4

5

AFRICA

6

3

1

7

2

ASSES

1 Mongolia – dzeggetai
2 Turkmenia – kulan
3 Iran – onager
4 Tibet – kiang
5 India – khur
6 Somalia – Asiatic wild ass
7 Australia – feral burros
8 North America – feral burros

ZEBRAS

1 south and east Africa – plains
2 South Africa – mountain
3 Kenya – Grevy's

AUSTRALASIA

7 8

9

SEMI-WILD HORSES

1 Norway – Norwegian Fjord
2 Britain – Dartmoor, Exmoor, Lundy, New Forest, Shetland
3 Germany – Dülmen
4 France – Camargue

FERAL HORSES

1 Western North America – mustang
2 Sable Island, Canada – Sable Island
3 Assateague Island, USA – Assateague, Chincoteague
4 Argentina – Criollo
5 Poland – tarpan
6 Mongolia – Przewalski
7 Namibia – Namib Desert
8 Australia – brumby
9 New Zealand – Kaimanawa

▼ SURVIVORS IN INDIA

The last refuge of the khur, a subspecies of Asiatic wild ass, is an area of bleak desert called the Rann of Kachchh. It lies in Gujarat, in the northwest corner of India, near the border with Pakistan.

African Relationships

Some animals on the grasslands of Africa are good companions. Zebras often share grazing grounds and water with antelopes, gazelles and ostriches. There is safety in numbers and many eyes can spot danger more efficiently. Grevy's zebra stallions do not migrate in the dry season but stay to guard their territories. They team up with groups of oryx and giraffes. Lone plains zebra stallions may link up with Grevy's zebras, but rarely for long. When different species meet, however, there is a pecking order. At a water hole, plains zebras outrank gazelles and Grevy's zebras, but move aside for wildebeest, giraffes, rhinoceroses and even warthogs.

▶ WASH AND BRUSH-UP

The red-billed oxpecker offers an attractive service to zebras. The zebra stands with its legs widespread, drops its ears and lifts its tail. The bird can then pick off skin parasites, such as ticks, from the places where the zebra cannot reach. However, the birds are a mixed blessing, because they also peck at sores. This keeps the wounds open so that the birds can drink the zebra's blood.

◀ MUTUAL BENEFIT

Plains zebras drink side-by-side with other animals at a water hole. They may form mixed herds at prime grazing sites, too. This may be where territories of different species of animal overlap. Zebras often provide a service to more sensitive grazers. They mow through the strong, new vegetation, eating all the tough indigestible bits, and clearing a path.

▲ PREDATOR WATCH

A spotted hyena carries off a piece of a zebra that has been killed by a lioness. Hyenas, wild dogs and lions are the main enemies of zebras. A zebra that spots danger issues a warning call. Mothers and foals hide behind other members of the group. A zebra stallion will attack a hyena with its hooves. If any zebra should break ranks and flee, then the rest run too.

▲ MIGRATION HAZARDS

A huge Nile crocodile has grabbed a plains zebra as it crosses the Mara River in Kenya. The crocodile holds the zebra in its strong jaws and pulls it under the water. Once it has drowned, the crocodile will twist off bite-sized pieces to eat.

▶ MEAL FOR A KING

This feral horse in the Kalahari Desert probably died of natural causes. The male lion is scavenging rather than hunting. Adult lions, with their heavy manes, are no match for a fleet-footed horse. Lionesses do hunt equids, and are often successful.

◀ FLY-BORNE DISEASE

The tsetse fly attacks most warm-blooded animals in southern and eastern Africa, but ignores zebras. The secret is in the stripes. In research with dummy zebra shapes, ones that were plain white or black were targeted by the flies. The striped shapes were ignored. It is thought that the insect's compound eyes, made up of lots of tiny lenses, cannot see the zebra as a body because of the stripes.

The Journey of

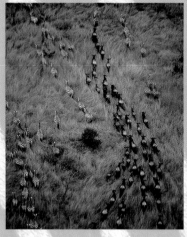

Vast herds of zebra, gazelles and wildebeest live on the plains of south and east Africa. They are constantly on the move, searching for better areas of grazing. The herds migrate from the acacia thorn forests in the northwest to the grasslands in the southeast, and back again. Their circular trip takes a year.

Zebras can sense a rainstorm from up to 60 miles away. They gather into large herds to watch for rain clouds and listen for thunder. The rain fills waterholes and ensures plenty of fresh, new grass. Zebras are the first to arrive in these areas. They feed on the toughest parts of the vigorous new vegetation, paving the way for the more delicate grazers that follow.

1 From July to September, hundreds of thousands of animals follow the rains from the Serengeti towards the Masai Mara. They move in long columns, following the same, well-worn paths every year.

2 One of the major obstacles on the great migration is the Mara River. No animal wants to take the plunge and cross first. Enormous numbers of zebras and their traveling companions, wildebeest and gazelles, build up on the riverbank.

the Zebras

3 When one animal starts to cross, the rest follow quickly. If the river is swollen by the rains, the animals must swim. Some are swept away in the torrent. Smaller members of the herd are pulled down and drowned by crocodiles. If the river is low, the zebras can wade across. They are quite capable of kicking an attacking crocodile with their hind feet and escaping.

4 Lionesses from a resident pride watch and wait among zebra and topi that have crossed the river. They will pounce on any floundering animal. The migrating animals offer a seasonal glut of food as they pass through the lions' territory.

5 The zebras have panicked at the scent of lions nearby and they abandon their river crossing. They will head back onto the plains, regroup and return to the river to try again. Somehow the zebras must cross to get to the new grass on the other side.

6 A lioness chases a scattered herd of zebra and antelope. The pride has fanned out and encircled the herd, chasing them towards an ambush. The migrating animals are followed by hyenas and nomadic lions on the lookout for stragglers and unprotected youngsters.

Running Free

All over the world, horses have escaped from enclosures or have been released from failed farms and ranches. Often the horses have not only survived, but have thrived and multiplied.

Most feral horses are not considered to be owned, but some herds are looked after by people who are concerned about their survival. Occasionally, a government agency may decide that a population of feral horses is out of control. They might be upsetting the balance of wildlife or damaging the environment. A cull might be ordered. The horses are rounded up. Some are killed while others may be sold to be domesticated once again.

▲ WHOSE HORSES?

Brumbies get their name from James Brumby, a soldier who arrived in Australia in 1791. He owned horses in New South Wales but then moved to Tasmania and left the horses behind. When people asked who owned the horses, the reply was "they're Brumby's." These two live on Fraser Island off the coast of Queensland.

▼ EVOLUTION IN ACTION

This Argentinian feral mare and her foal are probably descended from Spanish horses. There may be quite a range of sizes and colors in their herd because their Spanish ancestors were of different breeds. The fittest survived, and gradually the feral horses became better adapted to local conditions.

◄ ISLAND LIFE

The range of Sable Island horses is limited by the barrier of the sea. When concentrated into such small areas, herds of feral horses may overgraze the land and upset the ecosystem. Sable Island is off Nova Scotia.

FERAL BURROS ▼

In Australia and North America, asses were used as pack animals by miners and prospectors in the gold rushes of the late 1800s. They were turned loose and survived with great success in the wild. In Australia, about 1.5 million feral asses are running wild.

◄ MIXED BLESSING

About 300 feral ponies live on the island of Assateague off Maryland. They are said to have landed there in 1600, when a Spanish galleon sank offshore. The ponies eat grasses, rosehips, bayberry and saltwater grass, but are threatening the delicate marshland ecology.

ON THE RUN ►

Mustang territories are limited by human habitation, but the horses do not always respect the boundaries. They may breed with ranch horses and reduce the quality of the stock, or damage crops. In such situations, they are culled. Feral horses have few natural predators because of their size and ability to run from danger.

Living Semi-wild

There are some wild places in the world where horses can roam free for most of the year. They do have owners, however, and once a year, they are rounded up. Otherwise, the semi-wild horses live just like their truly wild relatives, forming herds and foraging for food. Semi-wild horses were specially bred to survive in the local climate and vegetation, and have been kept in the same area for many generations. The round-up takes place when the foals are a few months old, usually in the autumn. The owners check the health of their animals, brand new foals, and select some of the animals to break in and sell.

▲ TINY BUT TOUGH
Shetland ponies can withstand the harsh weather in the north of the British Isles. They have thick coats and large nostrils to warm the cold air before it enters their lungs. Their high-stepping walk makes it easier to negotiate the rough ground.

▲ HOME ON THE RANGE
Ponies have lived in the New Forest in southern England for over 1,000 years. Each social group has its own home range, which must include food and water supplies, and a "shade". Shades are usually open spaces where animals gather in hot weather to find some relief from insects.

▲ GERMAN HERD
Dülmen ponies live in Westphalia, Germany. Herds of semi-wild ponies have lived here since the 1300s. The Dülmen is not considered to be a pure breed because animals from Britain and Poland have been introduced into the herd.

TRADITIONAL HAIRCUT ▶

These are Norwegian Fjord ponies. The pony on
the left has been broken for riding, but has been
turned out to run free for the summer. While
under human control, its mane was cut short in
the traditional fashion. It will soon grow back to
its natural state, as on the pony on the right.

◀ DO NOT FEED THE PONIES!

Some semi-wild horses live in areas also
visited by tourists and crossed by roads.
Although people are asked not to feed
the ponies, this does happen. The horses
supplement their grazing with leftovers
from tourist picnics. But they have little fear
of cars and many are killed on the roads.

SINGLE FILE ▶

Dartmoor ponies came close
to extinction 60 years ago.
The horses have lived on
Dartmoor, in southwest
England, for 1,000 years.
Today, mares run free on the
moor but pedigree stallions
have been introduced to
improve the breed.

◀ SELECTED FEW

On the tiny island of Lundy, off the
southwest coast of England, lives a
group of about 30 ponies. It is
divided into two herds, one living
on the island's exposed plateau, and
the other on the more protected
farmland area. Lundy Island
ponies are a recognized breed.

43

Tough Horses

A corner of southwest Africa is home to the only horses in the world known to live in hot desert conditions. The feral horses of the Namib Desert are thought to have come from Europe and escaped from their owners over 80 years ago. The animals were not disturbed by anyone, because diamonds were found in the area and entry was restricted. They have not always thrived, however, and have been close to the brink of extinction. A security officer with the diamond mines spotted the horses in the 1970s. He raised the necessary funds to provide them with a permanent water supply. The Namib population once reached a peak of 280 individuals. Today, it is smaller—about 150-160 animals—one of only two or three groups of feral horses in Africa.

WATCH THEM PLAY

Scenes such as this can be enjoyed by tourists. A blind has been set up so that people can watch the Namib Desert horses. Conservationists are divided about the horses. Some want them protected, while others want to cull them so that they do not damage the fragile desert environment.

DRINKING IN THE DESERT

Water is in short supply in the Namib Desert. The horses must trek to an artificial borehole to drink. The desert horses are smaller than the horses from which they supposedly descended. They also urinate less, and can go without water for up to five days.

of the Desert

UPS AND DOWNS OF DESERT LIFE

The Namib horses are bony and unkempt, but they have survived against all odds. They live alongside specialized desert animals such as the gemsbok, oryx, ostrich and springbok. Because of their isolation in a hot, dry desert, the horses are relatively free of diseases and parasites.

BABY BOOM

The horses fatten up and breed when the rains come and food is more plentiful. Because the herds are small and isolated, the animals only breed with each other. Scientists are interested in studying the effects of such inbreeding.

SAND BATHING

Rolling in sand is one way horses keep their coats in tip-top condition. The unique environment of the Namib horse might also be useful to scientists trying to understand how animals cope with extreme climate change.

ESSENTIAL RAIN

The Namib horses are thin for most of their lives, but they grow fatter and the population swells in years of good rains. The sudden growth of desert plants provides them with an instant food bonanza.

Early Ancestors

The earliest horselike creatures were the size of a fox. They appeared on Earth about 54 million years ago. There was not much change in the equine body for the next 20 million years. Legs became longer, though, making flight from predators and long-distance travel easier.

Then, grassland vegetation evolved. Earlier species had lived in forests and browsed on woody plants and trees. The new food supply triggered many different horselike species to evolve. The ones that survived best in the open grasslands were those with the longest legs and biggest bodies. Less than two million years ago, the one species that was to survive as the modern horse evolved. It was called *Equus* (from which we get the word equestrian).

Early horses had digits like human fingers and toes. To help the horse run faster, these gradually reduced to the single digit of the hoof.

▲ **ECHOES OF THE PAST**
Przewalski's horse is similar in appearance to the original *Equus* species. The body is short and stocky, the head is large and there is a dark strip along the spine.

▼ **EVOLUTION AND SURVIVAL**
Biologists often use the development of the horse to teach evolution because there are so many prehistoric horse fossils. Many different branches of horse evolved from around 20 million years ago (mya), but only *Equus*, ancestor of the modern horse, survived. *Equus* died out in America because of climatic changes at the end of the Ice Age. Its domestication by humans in Asia saved it from extinction.

Hyracotherium
54 mya

Mesohippus
30 mya

Merychippus
20 mya

Equus
2 mya

▶ FLAT-FOOTED ANCESTOR

One of the earliest fossil horses is *Hyracotherium* or *Eohippus*. It was no bigger than a dog and was a general plant eater. It had four digits on its front foot and three on the hind foot, and ran on the flat of its feet rather than on its toes.

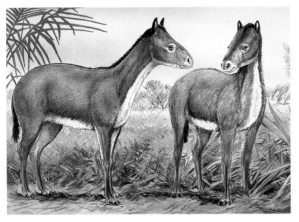

◀ BROWSING EXPERT

Mesohippus appeared 38–25 mya. Its forefoot had three digits, and it was bigger than *Hyracotherium*. The chewing surface of its teeth increased so that it could browse more efficiently on the shoots and leaves of trees and shrubs.

VICTIM OF SUCCESS ▶

The three-toed horse, *Anchitherium*, was one of many horselike creatures that evolved 25-5 mya. It invaded Eurasia from North America but became extinct and had no descendants. It may have become very well adapted to a particular environment. When that environment disappeared, due to climatic change, *Anchitherium* died out.

◀ GRASSLAND INHABITANT

The great expansion of savannah grassland around 20 mya in North America gave rise to horses such as *Merychippus*. The browsers were still around, but new species evolved that were specially adapted to grassland vegetation and open country. Their legs and stride became longer, and the back strengthened, so that they could flee from danger.

How the Horse was Tamed

Early people hunted wild horses for food. They did not capture and breed from them until about 6,000 years ago—and then only for meat and milk. This was many hundreds of years after sheep and goats had been domesticated. Fossils of horse teeth worn down by a bit prove that horses were first ridden 5,500–6,000 years ago. Imagine how brave the first person to try riding the power-packed wild horse must have been! Farmers from central Asia were the first to do it, and all modern horses are descended from their small, stocky mounts. Since then, though, humans have bred many types of horses for different jobs, from fast, light breeds for riding to heavy draft animals.

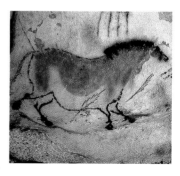

▲ **LASCAUX HORSES**
The cave paintings at Lascaux in France are about 15,000 years old. They feature horses that resemble Przewalski's horse. Small populations of wild horses survived in Europe until about 2500B.C.

▲ **FIGHTING HORSE POWER**
Horses helped win many battles through history. Horse-drawn war chariots date from 1800B.C., and cavalry developed as a fighting force from about 1000B.C. Mounted warriors could move quickly and, from their higher level, could cut down foot soldiers easily.

▲ **HEAVYWEIGHTS**
Clydesdales helped bring the North American prairies and the newly settled land of Australia under cultivation. They hauled plows through heavy soil and pulled fully loaded wagons. Clydesdales weigh about one ton, but they are one of the lighter draft breeds.

◄ RIDING SAFELY

Pony trekking is a long way from the time when the spirited wild horse was first mounted on the Asian steppes. Horses must be carefully schooled to overcome their natural nervousness.

CEREMONIAL HORSE ►

Today, military horses rarely go into battle, but are still ridden in ceremonies. These horsemen are wearing jodhpurs, breeches named after the city of Jodhpur in India, which was an equestrian center.

Biblical Transport

Horses play important parts in Jewish and Christian holy texts. The prophet Elijah was transported to Heaven in a fantastic burning chariot. Enoch, who was chosen by God to be king of the angels, was carried in a storm chariot pulled by six chargers. In ancient times, horses were connected with luxury and nobility.

▼ NATURAL SPORT

Humans want to breed horses that can win jumping competitions and races. In the wild, the strongest and fastest horses evolve naturally as they are the most likely to survive. Humans select and breed from previous winners. Horses seem to enjoy many sports that humans impose upon them. It may be because these sports are similar to how horses play naturally.

Zebras and Stripes

There are three living species of zebra – the plains zebra (which is also known as the common zebra or Burchell's zebra), the mountain zebra and Grevy's zebra. Each species has a distinctive stripe design, and the pattern varies with each animal. It is possible that zebras within a herd recognize each other by familiar patterns. The ancestors of all equids probably had stripes like the zebra.

No one knows exactly what purpose the stripes serve. They are unlikely to be a form of camouflage, as zebras never hide from their enemies. However, the stripes do make the animals hard to see at dawn, dusk and by moonlight, which are the main times of rest. They may also deter biting insects from landing. Another theory is that the two-tone combination may help regulate heat in the animal's body—white reflects heat and black absorbs it.

▲ **IDENTITY STRIPE**
The northern herds of the plains zebra have bolder stripes than those in the south. The variation may be to do with the way the different herds organize themselves. Generally, zebras with the boldest stripes tend to form large groups at seasonal sources of food in grasslands.

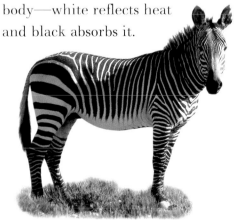

▲ **MOUNTAIN PATTERN**
The mountain zebra has close-set stripes, which become very broad on the top of its rump. Its numbers have decreased, and it is only found in reserves in southwest Africa.

▲ **ORIGINAL PINSTRIPE**
Grevy's zebra has the narrowest stripes of the three zebra species. It is the most primitive, too, similar to the ancestor of all zebras that evolved five million years ago.

▲ SAFETY IN NUMBERS

A group of plains zebras has many pairs of nostrils, eyes and ears to detect danger. They form social herds, protected by a stallion. Grevy's zebras, however, do not form social herds. Lone stallions guard territory and are vulnerable to predators.

▶ GROWING UP FAST

Ten minutes after this plains zebra foal was born, it could stand. It could walk after 20 and canter after 45. Newborn zebras must be able to run from predators almost immediately.

◀ SALTY SNACK

One or two animals keep watch while the others enjoy a salt lick—where salt occurs in rocks. In hot countries, mammals need to replace the salt they lose through sweat. Even when zebras lie down to sleep at night, one or two remain on lookout duty.

Asses and Donkeys

The toughness, strength and sure-footedness of the African wild ass were noticed by humans about 6,000 years ago. People living in the Middle East quickly put their discovery to good use. They tamed some of the animals and put them to work. The domestic donkey is the descendant of these asses.

Donkeys have been used as pack (carrying) animals for centuries. While neither as speedy nor as elegant as other equids, the donkey can work under hot, difficult conditions. It is sturdy, keeps going for days on very little food, and can carry 225 pounds in weight. It can also travel without water for much longer than a horse.

The Asiatic wild ass has several subspecies, such as the onagar and the kiang. Each population is isolated and lives a considerable distance from its close relatives.

▲ OUT OF AFRICA
The Somali wild ass is one of the world's most endangered mammals. Just a few scattered groups survive in Somalia and Ethiopia. The asses sometimes breed with domestic and feral donkeys, which is also a threat to the wild population. It is hard to know which are pure Somali wild asses and which are hybrids.

▼ INDIAN SURVIVOR
Khurs are a subspecies of the Asian wild ass. They live in a desert in the north-west of India, grazing on the sparse grass. There used to be thousands of khurs on the arid plains, but many have died from diseases caught from domestic cattle.

▲ FLEETEST OF FOOT

The flat, desert country of Kachchh, in India is ideal for making a fast escape. Khurs are the swiftest of all wild equids. They are quite capable of reaching speeds of 45 miles per hour for brief periods and attaining a sustained speed of 30 miles per hour over long distances. Like other equids, their main defence is speed.

▼ HOLDING ON TO WATER

Asses, such as this one from Somalia, are remarkable for their ability to live in the desert. They can survive water losses that are 30 percent of their body weight. Most other mammals would die after losing 12-15 percent. Asses can restrict sweating and reduce the water content of their droppings. When they reach water they can drink enough—25-30 quarts— to restore water loss in two to five minutes.

Abdul of Gallipoli

A Greek donkey called Abdul became a First World War hero. He accompanied a stretcher bearer at the terrible battle of Gallipoli in 1915. The two of them carried hundreds of injured Australian soldiers to safety, often under fire. When the stretcher bearer was killed, Abdul continued the dangerous trek alone.

▼ USEFUL DONKEY

In early days, the donkey was not only used for transport. In ancient Egypt, it trod seeds during the threshing of grain, and mares were milked. Donkey mares' milk has a higher sugar and protein content than cows' milk and was used by the ancient Egyptians for food, medicine and as a cosmetic for the skin.

Brought Back to Life

▲ HORSE OR ZEBRA?
The quagga looked like a cross between a zebra and a horse. It had stripes on its forequarters, like a zebra, while hindquarters were plain, like a horse.

In the past few centuries, several breeds of equids have become extinct because of over-hunting, or the destruction of their habitat. But it is now possible to recreate extinct species for release back into the wild. Scientists in South Africa are breeding an extinct zebra subspecies called the quagga, which died out over 100 years ago. They analyzed DNA from the cells of a quagga skin in a museum and compared it to other zebra species. The quagga is a subspecies of the plains zebra. Suitable plains zebras with paler stripes were selected to start a breeding program to bring the quagga back to life.

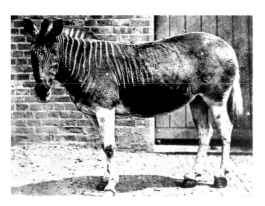

▲ SWIFT DECLINE
The quagga lived in a barren area of South Africa. Early settlers thought it competed with their sheep and goats for the sparse grass. Millions were slaughtered, many simply for sport. Some quaggas were transported to zoos. Breeding was not thought necessary because everyone believed there were plenty of the animals in the wild. The last quagga died in Amsterdam Zoo on 12 August 1883.

▲ SLOW BUT SURE
Nine plains zebras like this one were chosen for the Quagga Project. In 1998, descendants of these nine were released in Karoo National Park. They are the only zebras there so will only breed among themselves. The ones in each generation that are most quagga-like are selected for the next stage of breeding. It is a long process because it takes two to three years for a zebra to become sexually mature.

◄ ORIGINAL COPY

One of the zebras from the Quagga Project shows that it is losing its plains zebra stripes, is browner, and more quagga-like. Eventually, a foal will be born that matches the appearance of the extinct animal exactly.

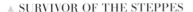

▲ **SURVIVOR OF THE STEPPES**

The konik pony (above) comes from Poland. It is a descendant of the tarpan (*Equus przewalski gmelini*), a primitive pony that survived in the wild until the 1800s. The tarpan lived on the high steppes of eastern Europe and western Asia. The tarpan's genetic makeup was identified by looking at the konik and others of its descendants. A breeding program like the one recreating the quagga was set up.

▲ **BACK TO THE WILD**

The Polish government are trying to recreate the tarpan. They released Przewalski's stallions (above) and tarpan-like mares, such as koniks and Icelandic horses, into two Polish nature reserves. Today, horses almost identical to the tarpan run wild there. Tarpans were a victim of their own success. The stallions were fierce fighters and could take over harems of different breeds. This diluted the tarpan breed.

Close Relatives

The closest relations to horses are other hoofed animals, known as ungulates (from the Latin word for nail). Closer relations still are the ungulates with an odd number of toes. Have you noticed that the hooves of cows, goats and sheep are split, or cloven into two equal parts? They are even-toed ungulates. The horse, with its single hoofed toe, is related to two other odd-toed ungulate families—the rhinoceroses and the tapirs.

About 40 million years ago, the odd-toed ungulates were the dominant hoofed animals in North America, and they spread throughout much of the world. The animals adapted to eat different foods. Huge, giraffe-like animals browsed on fruit in the treetops, early horses fed at the middle levels and rhinos ate the fiberous shoots and leaves at the bottom. Gradually, most of the families died out, having succumbed to hunting or disease, or because of climate change. Of the survivors, the rhinoceroses are endangered and at risk of disappearing altogether, like their ancient ancestors.

▲ GREAT GRAZERS
All odd-toed ungulates (hoofed animals) are vegetarian. Horses and the white rhino are grazers, feeding mostly on grass. Other rhinos and tapirs are browsers, selecting more nutritious food, such as fruit, seeds and leaves.

◄ A QUESTION OF TOES
Rhinos leave tracks that look like a clover leaf or an ace-of-clubs in the dust. Unlike the equids, rhinos still have three toes. *Mesohippus*, the prehistoric ancestor of both the horse and the rhinoceros, had three toes on each foot. As the horse evolved into a specialized runner, it lost two toes, leaving a single, hoofed digit.

◄ TIMID TAPIR

Tapirs forage for food with their short, mobile trunk. They hide in thick vegetation by day, and come out at night to bathe and feed. They often cover their short dense coats with mud as protection against insect bites. Tapirs live in tropical and sub-tropical forests in South America and Malaysia. They have three toes on their back feet and four on the front.

► UNDER THREAT

This black rhino baby is very precious. In the last few decades, the rhino population of east Africa has been drastically reduced by hunting and the destruction of their habitat. Black rhinos produce only one calf every three years. It will take a long time for the population to recover.

◄ SPECIALITY MOUTHS

Look at the broad, square lips of these white rhinos. They are a clue to its feeding habits. White rhinos are specially designed for cropping the grasslands of south and northeast Africa. Black and Asian rhinos have prehensile (capable of grasping), pointed lips for browsing. All rhinos have a digestive system like that of a horse. Food is broken down by bacteria in an enlarged hind gut.

57

▲ RIVER HORSE

Hippos love bathing in water.
Their name comes from the
ancient Greek words for horse
and river. Like horses, they
graze on grasses. Hippos feed
at night, plucking the grass
with their broad lips.

▶ HIGH LIVING

Giraffes browse the tops of trees
where no other herbivores can
reach. Their prehensile
(grasping) lips and tongues are
even more mobile than
those of horses. They
pick out tasty leaves
from among
thorns.
Their ears
are very
mobile
too.

Fellow Plant Eaters

Many other ungulates (hoofed animals) are
grazers like the equids, but they have an even
number of weight-bearing toes instead of a
single hoof. These even-toed ungulates are found
in almost every habitat and on every continent
except Australia and Antarctica. They also digest
their food quite differently from equids. Most of
them are cud-chewing ruminants, such as
giraffes, antelope, camels, cattle and sheep. A
second group, which includes hippopotamuses
and pigs, are non-ruminants.

Even-toed ungulates were the
main animals of the grasslands
where the first humans evolved.
They were captured and bred for
their milk, meat and hides.

▲ TINY PUDU

The pudu of South America is the world's
smallest deer. It lives in beech forests, feeding
on fruit and other vegetation. The pudu can
give us some idea of how *Hyracotherium*,
the first ancestor of the horse, lived.

▲ TRAVELING COMPANION

The wildebeest, or gnu, are grazers of the African plains, like the zebras. Vast numbers of wildebeest follow the zebra herds on their annual migrations. Wildebeest are members of the antelope family, like the gazelles. They are noisy animals, with a range of bleats, grunts and snorts. Young bulls will often lock horns in mock fights.

▲ VARIED DIET

Warthogs feed almost entirely on grasses. After the rains, they pluck the growing tips with their incisor teeth or their lips. At the end of the rains they eat grass seeds, and in the dry season they use the hard upper edge of their nose to dig up roots. Warthogs live in family groups in the open country of Africa.

▼ HIGH-SPEED GAZELLE

Herds of Thomson's gazelles range the African savannahs. Every large predator tries to catch them, but like horses, gazelles rely on speed to escape. They can keep up speeds of 40 miles per hour for more than 15 minutes.

▼ FIGHTING HORNS

Male bighorn sheep, like other ruminants, make use of their horns when defending their territory or their females. Horses never developed horns because their way of fighting relies on agility and biting more than strength. Bighorn sheep have adapted to a wide range of habitats in North America, from desert to chilly alpine areas. As they bound swiftly over rocky ground, their padded feet grip and absorb the shock of impact.

Conservation

While domestic breeds of horses and asses multiply, their wild cousins fight for survival. The only wild equid that is still plentiful and occupying its natural range is the plains zebra in Africa. The others live in small isolated groups, and many are in danger

of extinction. Some are bred in zoos and then returned to the wild in protected reserves.

Feral horses and asses are also in danger. They may be considered pests and are shot or poisoned. The feral burro (ass) in North America is blamed for the decline of native bighorn sheep. They damage the topsoil and compete with the sheep for food and water. Nevertheless, the burro is protected by law, and charities have been set up to help the free-ranging herds.

▲ **RETURN TO THE WILD**
Przewalski's horse once lived in the Altai Mountains of Mongolia, but it has not been seen in its natural habitat since 1968. Before it became extinct, 13 were brought into captivity and bred in zoos all over the world. Now their descendants are being returned to the wild. Sixty horses have been reintroduced in a specially created mountain steppe reserve in Mongolia.

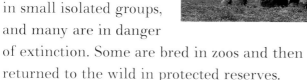

◀ **UPSETTING THE BALANCE**
Cumberland Island horses, like all feral herds living on islands off the east coast of North America, may upset the delicate island ecology. Birdwatchers say the horses should be removed as they are not natural. The National Parks Service protects the horses. There is a rich range of wildlife on these islands, including feral hogs.

◀ CONTROLLING NUMBERS

Chincoteaguen feral horses are kept at the Virginia end of Assateague Island off the east coast. They are kept separate from the Assateague ponies, another feral group on the island. The Chincoteague Volunteer Fire Company keeps the herd to below 150. By doing this, they hope to lessen damage to the island ecology. Each year, some Chincoteague ponies are sold to help pay for the upkeep of the feral herd.

▶ NEAR THE BRINK

The onager is one of the smallest, fastest and nimblest equids. It is a subspecies of the Asiatic wild ass and lives in northern Iran. Intense hunting caused a huge population decline, and many were pushed from their habitats by fighting in World War I. Recently, the onagers numbers have been increasing.

▲ PROTECTED MUSTANGS

Life is not always easy for feral mustangs. They must survive harsh winters in the mountains. In many states, humans keep a watchful eye on them, and herds are protected by government organizations.

▲ NEW GENERATION

A feral foal has the chance of a more natural life than its domesticated cousins. But horses are one of the animals that have thrived under humans. There are about 60 million domestic horses in the world, far more than could be supported naturally.

GLOSSARY

ancestor
An ancient animal from which a more modern animal is directly descended.

Arab
A breed of horse which has a history going back 5,000 years.

bit
The bar placed in a horse's mouth that enables a rider to control it.

breed
A type of animal with specific characteristics that has been bred by people for a certain purpose, such as speed or strength.

browser
Plant-eating animal that feeds on bushes and trees.

caul
The protective membrane that surrounds a foal in the womb.

colt
Young male horse up to the age of four.

cull
To kill many animals in a controlled way.

descendant
The children, grandchildren, great-grandchildren or other direct offspring of an animal.

digestive tract
The tube that runs through the length of an animal's body that allows it to absorb nutrients from food. It is divided up into specialized sections, such as the stomach and intestine, which perform specific functions.

DNA
The basic genetic code, found in every cell in the body, to build the entire animal.

domestication
The taming and selective breeding of animals in order to supply human needs.

draft horse
A strong horse that pulls a cart or wagon with a heavy load.

equids
Horses and horselike animals, such as asses and zebras.

estrus
The time during which female mammals are receptive to mating because their eggs are ready for fertilization.

evolution
The natural change of living organisms over very long periods of time.

feral
Domestic animals that have escaped or been abandoned and are now living freely in the wild.

filly
Young female horse that has not yet bred.

flehmen
A behavior shown by many male mammals, during which they curl their lips back and smell the air, searching for important odors. Female equids and young horses also sometimes use the flehmen response.

fodder
Food for domestic animals.

forequarters
The front legs and shoulders of an equid.

gait
The way an animal moves at certain speeds. It refers to the order in which an animal moves its legs.

gene/genetic
The code for a physical trait and the way this is passed from one generation to another. Each gene contains a strand of DNA that is responsible for a feature, such as blue eyes.

grazer
An animal that eats low-growing plants, such as grasses and herbs.

groom
The way an animal cares for its coat and skin. It can be carried out by the animal itself or by one animal for another.

habitat
The particular place where a group of animals lives.

harem
A collection of females overseen by a single male.

herbivores
Animals that only eat plant food.

hindquarters
The back legs and rear part of an animal.

incisor teeth
A mammal's front teeth. Equids usually have six in the upper and six in the lower jaw.

joint
The structure where two bones fit together.

ligament
A strong band of fibrous tissue that squeezes between two bones in a joint. It ensures that the bones move without damage.

mare
Adult female horse.

migration
The regular, two-way movement of animals to and from feeding and breeding grounds.

molar teeth
The large cheek teeth used for crushing and grinding food.

nomadic
Constantly on the move in search of food and never staying for long in any one place.

nutrients
The goodness in foods that is essential for life.

parasites
Animals that live on other animals to the harm of their host. Fleas and ticks are parasites.

pedigree
Bred from known high-quality animals of a recognized breed.

pony
A small horse under 56 inches high.

prehensile
Able to grasp and maybe even manipulate objects. Horses' lips are prehensile.

prehistoric
The time before people began to record everyday events.

primitive
A horse that resembles the wild horses that lived before humans domesticated them. Primitive horses have a large head and a stocky body. They may have a stripe on their back or their legs.

semi-wild
Domestic animals that are left to run free over a large area of land for most of the year.

species
A group of animals that share similar characteristics and can breed together to produce fertile young.

stable herd
A group of equids, including horses and plains zebras, that form a permanent herd. Their bonds are to each other not a particular territory.

stallion
Adult male horse.

subspecies
A species is sometimes divided into smaller groups called subspecies. These occur in a particular area and are sufficiently different to have their own group. All animals of the same species are able to breed together.

tendons
The tough, fibrous tissue that joins muscle to bone.

thoroughbred
The world's fastest and most valuable breed of horse.

ungulate
A mammal with hooves.

INDEX